THE MARCHES IN PHOTOGRAPHS

BRYAN PHILLIPS

AMBERLEY

First published 2020

Amberley Publishing
The Hill, Stroud
Gloucestershire, GL5 4EP

www.amberley-books.com

Copyright © Bryan Phillips, 2020

The right of Bryan Phillips to be identified as the Author of this work has been
asserted in accordance with the Copyrights, Designs and Patents Act 1988.

ISBN 978 1 4456 8690 5 (print)
ISBN 978 1 4456 8691 2 (ebook)

British Library Cataloguing in Publication Data.
A catalogue record for this book is available from the British Library.

Typesetting by Aura Technology and Software Services, India.
Printed in the UK.

ACKNOWLEDGEMENTS

I am indebted to a number of people for their support in capturing many of the images in this book. My wife, Avril, is my inspiration, my guide and my gear-carrying companion for many of my journeys and treks through the county and beyond. She is the steadfast deliverer of lens and camera changes as I see and try to capture the time-bound images in front of me, always looking for a perfect shot. My eldest daughter, Lorraine (also a photographer), has been a stand-in when those early morning shots demand waking at 3 or 4 a.m. to travel to a site in the dark in order to capture those unique impressions of sunrise. Cheryl is my youngest and she keeps me in touch with the new technology and media developments such that I can successfully stay in touch with those who have followed my journey as Lightlog – with an aim to capture and replicate the light show that I see as I travel and note locations for future potential work.

This is my second publication with Amberley. The first, *Kent in Photographs*, has been very well received. The support I have received from friends, family and colleagues has encouraged me to expand my reach with this second book.

ABOUT THE PHOTOGRAPHER

Bryan Phillips is a proud Black Country man, growing up in the middle of the country among the steel-making industries the area is famed for. He has been the subject of a number of events showcasing his work, expressing his images through a variety of different media and formats.

'It's all about the light' is a frequent phrase used by Bryan, referring to the natural light element that is so important in building his images for reproduction. This knowledge brings the realisation that each location has a series of potential results depending on the immediate light conditions, and so a return to the same location builds a library of images that can look quite different. Being an 'early bird', sunrise is an important time for him, and you will see the results of some of these in the pages that follow.

In his daily life, Bryan is a marketing and sales professional in the technology industry, and this is where his association with the Welsh Marches began. Malvern was seen by the family as the perfect location to use as a base: it was within easy reach of South Wales and had a stunning location on hand in the Malvern Hills. As he will tell you, Bryan always has a camera at the ready as he travels through and around the county (as well as the world) – there are often opportunistic captures that await the ever-ready photographer. Of course, there are those shots that were missed when time pressures or mode of transport meant that a halt was not possible, even if only for a moment.

Bryan has successfully presented images for the BBC, a US backpacker's guide and various projects around the country, but he still enjoys the buzz of a gallery show where visitors often remark on the detail found in the canvases and prints on display.

Photography is my escape, my safe place, my creative release and I hope that you will be able to see some of that as you look through the images and notes in this book. I have been involved in photography from an early age, growing up with a Kodak Brownie bellows camera and developing my own images either in the loft or darkroom-converted bathroom. Modern equipment is much more versatile and allows high-quality images to be more frequently captured.

The images in this book have been captured using a variety of cameras, lenses and attachments, including:

Cameras: Nikon D850 / Nikon D800 / Nikon D810 / Nikon D700 / Nikon D300

Lenses: Nikkor AF-S 24–120 mm / Nikkor AF-S 16–35 mm / Nikkor AF-S 70–300 mm / Nikkor 200–500 mm

Accessories: Giottos MML3290B Monopod / Tiffen Filters

INTRODUCTION

The Marches often needs some initial explanation; in fact, the term itself is not completely clear. It may come from 'mark' or 'border', signifying a border between territories. In this case we are exploring the Welsh Marches. The border is not perfectly described, having moved quite a lot over a history of hundreds of years. A repeating theme centres around what we now know as Shropshire and Herefordshire, but we include a slightly wider definition for the images contained here.

As a border area, as you might expect, the area is littered with fortifications; however, there are more than just castles, with fortified houses and ancient hill forts dotted around the landscape too. Although named 'the Marches', in fact there is no reference to English marches in common use, therefore we are generally talking about the Welsh Marches here.

Following the Roman occupation of most of Britain, Wales consisted of a number of kingdoms. To fill the void of power after AD 410 the Angles and Saxons established their power bases in southern and eastern Britain, and after a time there was a quest to expand their territories further west. The boundary of Offa's Dyke signalled what would become the key frontier territory. Offa's Dyke can, of course, still be seen in the region.

After 1066 and the Norman Conquest, a few trusted nobles were installed to control this border territory. Hugh d'Avranches, Roger de Montgomerie and William FitzOsbern were given earldoms around the areas of Chester, Shrewsbury and Hereford. It was around this time that 'March of Wales' was first noted – it was used in the Domesday Book (1086). The marcher lords set up a number of controls along the border between the estuaries of the Severn in the south and the Dee in the north.

So we now come to 'Marchia Wallie', or the Welsh Marches, and by the twelfth century the term referred to something like two-thirds of what we know as Wales. Quite an extensive building programme was established in the next 200 years, evidence of which can be seen from examples as far north as Flint and Mold. This was very much seen as the Wild West of Britain until the Industrial Revolution.

The region around Ludlow and Hereford are seen as the centre of the Marches, and the council of Wales and the Marches had its centre of administration in Ludlow, first established in 1472 by Edward IV.

NORTHERN REACHES

Castles at Ewloe (shown here), Flint, Denbigh and Ruthin are evidence of the northern battleground of the border country between Wales and England. Being a border town Chester also has defences, and battlegrounds continue south towards Llangollen and Oswestry.

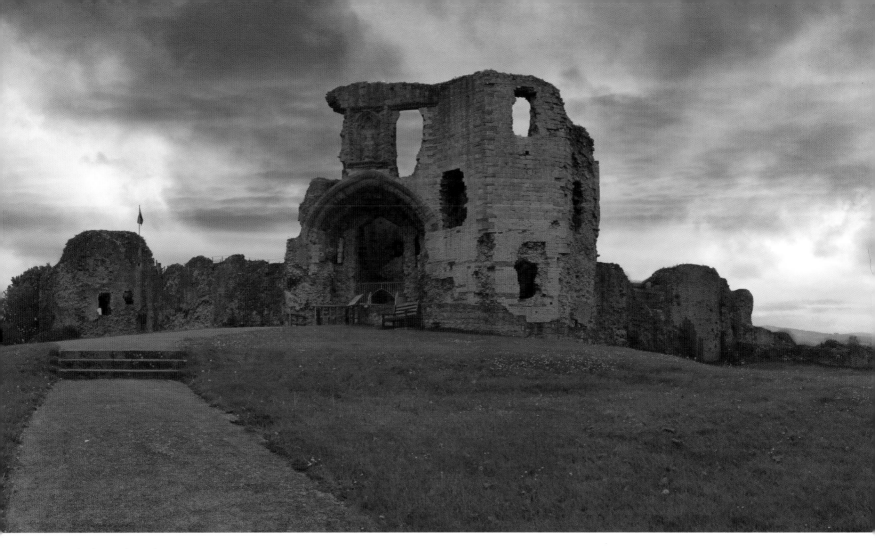

Denbigh Castle in the mist

Half-timbered buildings, Chester

River Valley, Clwydian Mountains

Coastal defences, Flint Castle

St Asaph Cathedral, the smallest cathedral in the UK

Inside St Asaph Cathedral

Horseshoe Falls, Llangollen

Rhuddlan Castle

Distant view, Clwydian Range

Shrewsbury skyline

Chester

Stanley Palace, half-timbered buildings, Chester

Chester Graving Dock and canal basin

Laura's Tower, Shrewsbury

Moody skies over the Long Mynd

The River Severn looking towards Ironbridge

Peeking through to Wroxeter Roman fort

Reclamation, Ludlow Castle

Ironbridge

Bottle kilns at Coalport China Museum

Sunrise over the River Severn at Ironbridge

Stained-glass window,
St Asaph Cathedral

Vintage bus, Chester

Old Dee Bridge, Chester

St Asaph, Britain's smallest cathedral

Half-timbered buildings, Eardisland

Early morning mist, River Clun

Stained-glass vision, Chester Cathedral

Eiseg's Pillar, Llantysilio

Hills and valleys at Horseshoe Pass, Llantysilio Mountain

Last light over a small range near Llangollen

Wroxeter Roman city ruins

HEARTLANDS

Shropshire and Herefordshire form the core of the Welsh Marches. Ludlow and Hereford have key places in history where power has been held from time to time. Ludlow in particular has possibly the best example of a fortified manor at Stokesay and is well worth a visit, including the church and the site of a battleground.

Floodplain, River Severn, Shrewsbury

Stairway to Heaven, British Camp, Malvern Hills

Reservoir, Herefordshire Beacon, Malvern Hills

Crepuscular rays over the fields of Herefordshire

Along the river, Bridgnorth

Sunset profile, Malvern Hills

Fortified manor house, Stokesay Castle

Ancient mark, Offa's Dyke

CLAWDD OFFA
OFFA'S DYKE

KING OF
MERCIA
757-796 A.D.

MARKING 80
MILES OF THE
BOUNDARY
OF WALES

"THE MOST IMPRESSIVE WORK
OF THE OLD ENGLISH KINGS"

OFFA'S DYKE ASSOCIATION 1971

Canopy, Clee Hills

Stokesay Church

British Camp and views towards Eastnor

Country house, Eardisland

It's a sign, Malvern Hills

Morning mist, Bridgnorth

The Old Schoolhouse, Acton Scott

Rest a while – Sir Edward Elgar, The Firs

The Coach House, Kington

The Long Mynd

British Camp, hill fort, Malvern

Villages and fields, view towards the Old Hills

Bathed at sunset, British Camp hill fort

Serenity at sunset, Colwall

Autumn gold, farmland around Wentnor

View from the ridge, Clee Hills

The setting sun on the edges of the Malvern Hills

Pinnacle Hill, Malvern

Half-timbered town
house, Ludlow

Shrewsbury Castle

Bluebell bonanza, Evendine Spring, Malvern Hills

Well dressed, Guarlford

M S P C A
1901

And so we stand together,
The horses, thee and me.
As the beasts take sips from the old stone trough
The world turns, quietly.

On the farm, Acton Scott

View from Manstone Rock, Stiperstones

Early light around Cathedral Precinct, Hereford

Lenticular clouds at sunset over the Malvern Hills

Spot the fields, Golden Valley

Ploughed patterns, Oswestry

Farm fragments, Acton Scott

A patchwork of fields, Herefordshire

Oswestry hill fort

St Chad's Church, Shrewsbury

Tracks and trails, Black Hill, Malvern

Clee Hill views

Hillside farms, Shropshire

The Dingle, Shrewsbury

Through the oval window, Clun

Timbers from history, Ledbury

Strolling, Long Mynd

Quiet little corner, Eardisland

Titterstone Clee Hill, near Ludlow

High Town, Bridgnorth

Ironbridge at sundown

St Mary Magdalene Church, Stretton Sugwas

Arthur's Stone, Dorstone

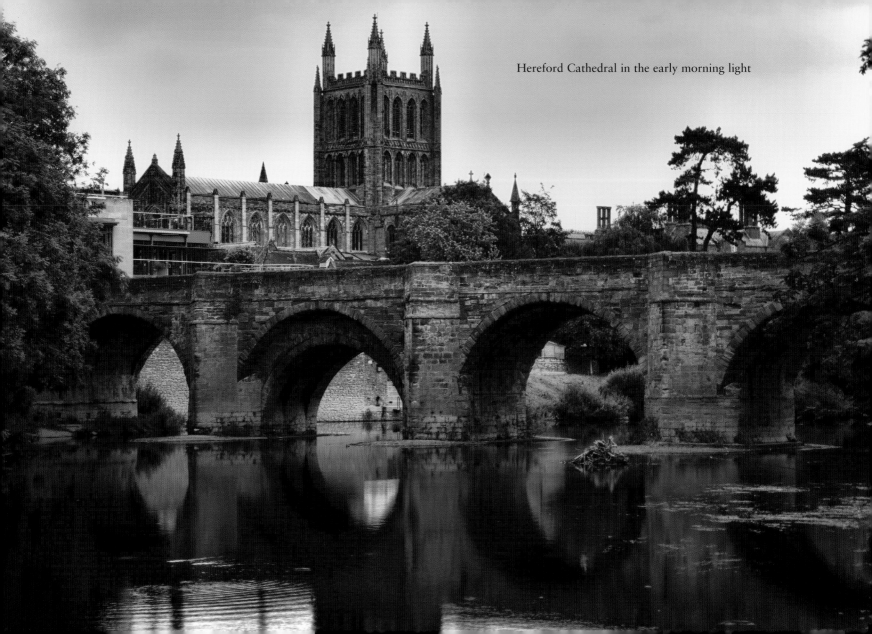

Hereford Cathedral in the early morning light

Market House, Ledbury

Border marking,
Offa's Dyke
Path, Clun

Stiperstones National Nature Reserve, Shrewsbury

Clun Castle ruins

Valleys and fields towards Carding Mill Valley

View from Manstone Rock, Stiperstones

SOUTHERN SHORES

Offa's Dyke stretches south towards the Severn Estuary. Along the way, continued evidence of fortifications and boundary lines between Wales and England continue to provide a rich history of the region.

Spanning the Wye, Symonds Yat

Sunrise over farmland, Llangeview

Evening tones, Ross-on-Wye

Watching stars, Raglan

Tintern Abbey

Chepstow Castle

Autumn fields, May Hill, Longhope

Shadows of morning, Monmouth

Severn Estuary

Parkland walk, Llanvihangel Gobion

Nature trail, Bishopswood

Borderline, Chepstow

Pastures new, Gilwern

Bridging the gap, Monmouth and Brecon Canal

Moored at sundown, Gilwern

Tranquil waters, Gilwern

The River Wye, Ross-on-Wye

Tintern Abbey

Chepstow Castle

Wooded slopes, Monmouth

...house, Llanfoist, Abergavenny